LOOM BEADING FOR BEGINNERS

The Complete Beginner's Loom Bead Weaving Guide with Pictures to Learn the Techniques, Patterns and Finishing to Create Stunning Jewelry, and Creating Your Own Patterns

JOANNA GAINES

Copyright @2022

COPYRIGHT © 2022 JOANNA GAINES

All rights reserved. No parts of this book may be reproduced, transmitted in any form or by any means – mechanical, electronic, photocopy, recording or any other except for brief quotations in printed reviews, without prior permission of the publisher.

Table of Contents

CHAPTER ONE 1
INTRODUCTION 1
CHAPTER TWO 4
MATERIALS, TOOLS, AND BASIC TERMINOLOGY 4
Tools and Materials.............. 4
Basic Loom Work Terminology 9
CHAPTER THREE 11
THE BEADING LOOMS 11
Selecting a Beading Loom Tips 13
How to Choose a Beading Loom 15
The Parts of a Bead Loom .. 17
Assembling the Loom 18
Threading the Loom 19
Frequently Asked 22

- CHAPTER FOUR 25
  - BEADING NEEDLES 25
    - Beading Needles Types 25
    - Choosing the Right Size Needles and Threads 32
      - For Size 15 Seed Beads ... 34
      - For Sizes 10 and 11 Seed Beads 36
      - For Size 8 Seed Beads 37
      - For Size 6 Seed Beads 38
    - Threading a Beading Needle 40
- CHAPTER FIVE 50
  - MISTAKES TO AVOID AS BEGINNERS 50
    - Using the Wrong Beads for a Project 50
    - Beading with Excessive Amount of Thread 53
    - Incorrect Beading Thread Tension 55
    - Splitting of Your Beading Thread 57

Being Scared of Trying New Beadwork Stitches 58

CHAPTER SIX 61
HOW TO USE A BEAD LOOM .. 61
- Supplies 61
- Instructions...................... 61

CHAPTER SEVEN.................... 87
COMPLETING YOUR WORK.... 87
- Slip Knots 87
- Decreasing....................... 88
- Fringing........................... 89
- Mounting Beadwork onto Other Material 91
- Joining Two Pieces of Beadwork 93
- Side Fringing.................... 95
- Selvage Method 97

CHAPTER EIGHT 111
BEAD LOOM PRACTICE PATTERN 111

Miyuki Bead Loom Cuff Bracelet........................ 111

Three Beaded Bracelet Patterns........................ 128

Make Your Own Pattern.... 129

CHAPTER ONE

INTRODUCTION

Bead looming is a simple and enjoyable method that originated as a Native American decorative art form many years ago. Looming has evolved over time, and contemporary beaders apply it regularly to produce trendy bracelets and accessories. The tools, materials, and equipment evolved along with the style and forms of using a bead loom. Using two- hole beads, leather cording, fibers, colorful patterns, and unique finishing options, you can simply spice up loomed designs.

Acquiring knowledge on how to operate a beading loom can significantly expand your craft range. These handy small tools let you make intricate and colorful beading designs to go with a variety of jewelry, fashion, and home décor projects. There's no vision you can't bring to life by beading on a loom, from intricate tribal patterns that pay homage to Native American original designs to exquisite florals and geometrics for your modern accessories.

Bracelets are among the most popular bead looming crafts. You may design colorful stacking bracelets or create bespoke patterns in your chosen shades. You may also create patriotic, nautical, and boho motifs with your bead loom.

You can create some of the most eye-catching crafts known to man with a relatively inexpensive loom, and your favorite beads!

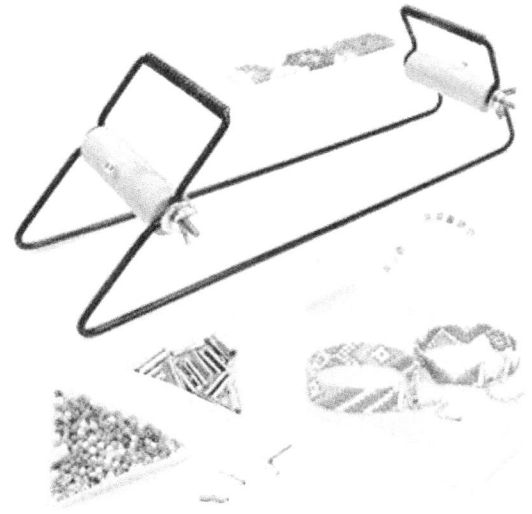

CHAPTER TWO

MATERIALS, TOOLS, AND BASIC TERMINOLOGY

Tools and Materials

Looming, like all art forms, necessitates a wide range of materials and tools. To have a pleasant crafting experience, make sure you have all of the necessary supplies on hand. If you're a seasoned beader, most of the essential supplies are likely already in your inventory; otherwise, they're readily available. Because there are so many different types, and brands of beading materials available, it's crucial to know which ones to use. Take, for example, thread. You can loom with nylon or braided beading threads, but there's a time and a place for each.

Seed Beads

Seed beads are frequently used with beading looms because their small size allows for more elaborate designs to be created over a smaller area. Of course, if the loom's warp spacing can be altered, larger beads can be employed.

Thread

The thread size you use will be determined by the size of the seed bead.

Needles

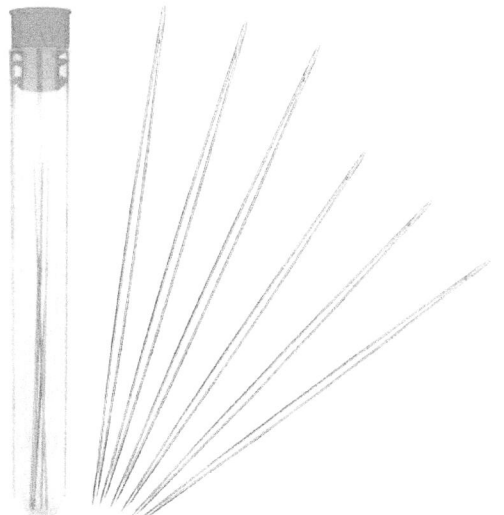

Any needle will do if it can get through the beads. A longer, less flexible needle, at least 3 inches long, is preferred by certain designers. It is determined by the width of your piece: long enough to contain the weft beads, plus enough for the tip and eye.

Patterns

Seed bead patterns show how the beads will be spread out row by row on the loom. Patterns of woven seed beads can be put together to make a bigger design.

Seed Bead Loom Kits

It's used to create a particular design, such as a brooch or a bracelet. Instructions, a stitch chart, beads, thread, and pin back are usually included with a beading loom kit. A beading loom, scissors, ruler, cellophane tape, and a beading needle are also required to finish the project.

Basic Loom Work Terminology

We won't have to go over all of the terms used in advanced weaving because we're dealing with simple looms.

Warp and Weft

Weaving words like warp and weft are rooted in history and tradition. These terms refer to the two directions of the thread on the loom. We don't need to know how the names came to be for our purposes; all we need to know is the difference. "Warp and down" (i.e., up and down), "weft and right" (i.e., left and right) is a mnemonic that will help you remember which thread goes up and down and which thread goes across. You can weave sideways on your loom, but the warp thread goes on first, and goes all the way across the loom.

CHAPTER THREE

THE BEADING LOOMS

A bead loom is an instrument for interlacing beads. A bead loom is a machine that weaves beads into a beaded fabric similar to cloth. It can be used to make flat strips of beadwork or larger beaded panels that can be put into purses, used as art, or added to larger items. The beads align in a row and column configuration in loom beading. Beading on a loom is faster than beading off the loom, but it takes a few extra steps to set up the loom before you can start.

A wide range of bead looms are on offer. All looms are designed to retain the warp threads under consistent tension to facilitate the weaving of beads on the weft threads. The length and number of warp threads will define the length and width of your finished product.

The advantage of bead looms is that you can use either a flat budget loom or a costly upright loom to weave beads successfully. Wireframe bead looms, wood frame fixed looms, adjustable frame bead looms, continuous warp bead looms, and upright bead looms have many similarities and distinctions. Choose the right loom for you, your beading project, and your budget.

Beading looms are used to manufacture jewelry, keychains, small purses, and other small beadwork crafts.

Selecting a Beading Loom Tips

1. **Size**: Beading looms are smaller than weaving looms, with a footprint of about a foot long, and several inches wide. They have different levels of portability.

2. **Construction**: Frames made of wood, plastic, or metal, as well as metal or plastic components like screws and thread stoppers (, or pegs) are on offer.

3. **Weaving Surface**: The maximum width and length you'll be able to weave with.

4. **Maximum Weaving Width**: The number of slots provided for holding threads running lengthwise.

5. **Benefit**: The characteristic or characteristics that describe what each loom has to provide, and differentiate one from another.

6. **Price**: Beading looms are available for about $10 to slightly over $50.

7. **Options for other bead sizes**: The intervals between threads on each loom can be altered to accommodate different bead sizes. Seed bead sizes range from 11 to 6 on most beading looms. Some can accommodate a seed bead of size 15.

How to Choose a Beading Loom

Tension

A quality bead loom should give uniform tension, which can ideally be adjusted as required. The ideal loom would have a warp tension controller and sled ends at the same height.

Durability

A stable foundation is essential for a positive bead loom experience. Look for sturdy plastic, metal, or wood construction materials. Additionally, you'll need a bead loom with enough weaving surface, and adjustability to accommodate different bead sizes.

Portability

Look for lightweight options with smaller dimensions if you enjoy crafting on the go. These mini bead looms are not only great for making small-scale crafts such as bracelets, ring toppers, pouches, and pendants; they are also great for jewelry-making parties.

The Parts of a Bead Loom

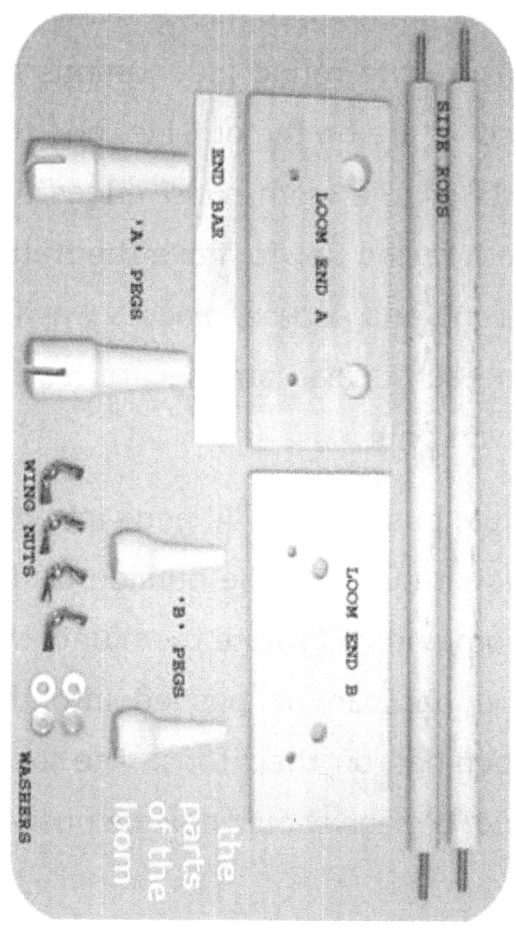

Assembling the Loom

Push the screw-threaded ends of the side rods through the smaller holes in loom ends 'A' and 'B'. Ensure the round indentations on end 'A' are on the outside, and the slits on the loom ends' edges are both facing up. To make the frame strong and secure, place a washer on each thread and secure it with a wing nut.

After pushing the 'A' pegs into the indentations on the outside of the loom end, 'A,' rotate them until the end bar can be pushed into the openings on their tops. The loom end 'B' pegs should now be pushed into the larger holes on the outside of the 'B' loom end.

The loom is now ready to be threaded or 'warped.'

Threading the Loom

Make a slip knot large enough to slide onto the end bar, on the end of the warping thread. Into its slot, replace the bar. Pass the thread through the corresponding slit on the other end of the loom, after sliding it between one of the slits on the loom end, and pulling it taut. Take the thread around the next 'B' peg and through the next slit on the loom end, keeping the tension tight. Return the thread to the other end and slide it through the next slit there as well. Return to the next slit in the series by passing the thread over the end bar once more.

Using a continuous length of thread, continue 'warping' the loom in this manner. Keep the thread taut at all times, and keep in mind that the number of warp threads necessary will be more than the number of beads in a row by one. For example, a piece of loomed work that needs to be 8 beads wide will require 9 warp threads. The warp thread can be firmly tied off to the next available peg after there are enough threads in place.

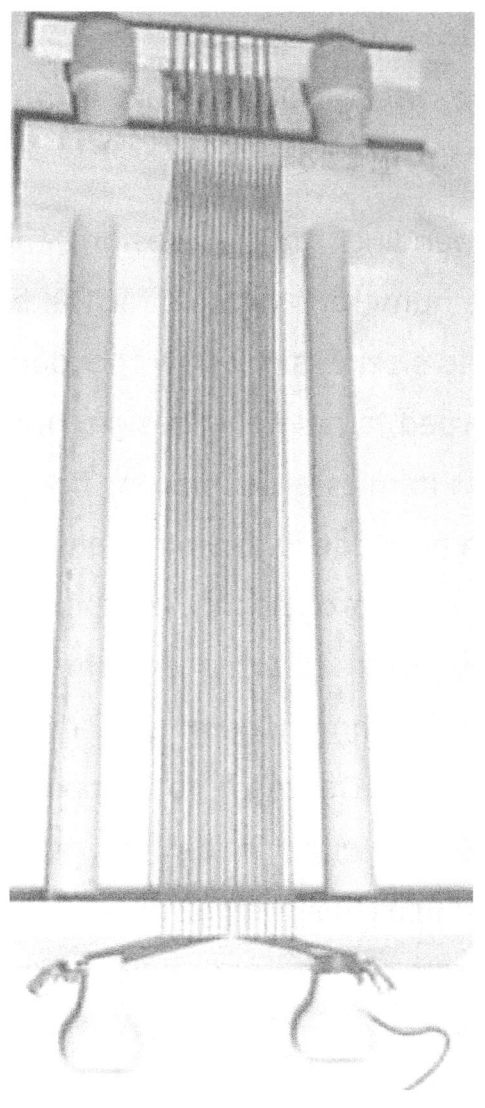

Frequently Asked

The Best Bead Size for a Beading Loom

Depending on the design, there are numerous options for the best bead size. Just by how the loom is warped, a painterly design, or one that mimics a painting or fine art, can be made with almost any bead size, regardless of whether it is woven, free form, or otherwise. It's recommended to use an 11/0 Miyuki Delicas for painterly designs with shade and depth. They have the most diverse color palette, color, and finish of any other size or form of bead on the market. To accommodate different bead sizes, utilize skip dents.

What is the Best Thread for Bead Looms?

Because the finished body of the item is carried by the warp thread, it's ideal to use a non-stretch thread for the warps. As far as color is concerned, the color of the thread will cause the bead colors to react differently, particularly translucent or silver-lined beads, and moss-green thread is nearly invisible in any color weave, including white.

What may a Bead Loom be used for?

A bead loom can be used to manufacture a wide variety of items. There is a lot that can be woven to wear or exhibit, including two-dimensional and three-dimensional beadwork, as well as free form and uniform designs. Earrings, bracelets, handbags, headbands, bookmarks, napkin rings, three-dimensional figures, and beaded creatures are just a few examples.

CHAPTER FOUR
BEADING NEEDLES

When dealing with tiny seed beads, the needle you use can make a great difference in how much fun you have beading.

When making beadwork, you should avoid using normal sewing or embroidery needles. They are convenient and affordable, but they are thicker, and their eyes are larger than needles designed just for beading.

Beading Needles Types

Selecting the appropriate size and type of beading needle will make your beadwork more fun and reduce the likelihood of broken beads and ruined work. There is a wide variety of variety when it comes to beading needles. Here are some of the most common ones: English, Japanese, bigeye, twisted, milliners, and glovers.

English Beading Needles

English beading needles are long, thin, flexible needles that are available in a variety of sizes to accommodate even the smallest seed beads. Beading needles of this type are the most prevalent. They're utilized for both loom and off-loom beading stitches like peyote, brick stitch, herringbone, netting, and others.

English beading needles are available in a variety of sizes. Size 10 or 12 needles are the most widely used needle sizes, and both work nicely with size 11/0 beads.

The type and size of beads you're using, the type and size of thread you're using, and the number of passes you'll need to make through the beads all influence the needle size you choose.

Craft stores, local bead stores, and online bead suppliers all have English beading needles. Beadsmith English Beading Needles and John James English Beading Needles are two brands to seek for.

Japanese Beading Needles

Thin, flexible needles with a strengthened eye and a gently rounded point characterize Japanese beading needles. Although they're more durable and more expensive, they are comparable to English needles in that they come in a variety of sizes.

Japanese beading needles are thin and flexible, making them ideal for loom and off-loom bead weaving. However, they do not bend or break as easily as English beading needles. When making numerous passes through a bead, the slightly rounded point reduces the chances of piercing the thread.

Bigeye Needles

Bigeye needles are exceptionally simple to thread. They feature a massive eye that runs the length of the needle.

Because they are constructed of two pieces of metal linked at the top and bottom, Bigeye needles are thicker than English beading needles. The center bows out when the needle is pushed from the ends, revealing the single enormous eye that runs the length of the needle.

Bigeye needles, which are readily available at most bead stores, are ideal for stringing projects, working with elastic cord, and other slightly thicker stringing materials. Big eye needles from BeadSmith and Beadalon are readily available. They're not the best choice for stitches that require repeated passes through a bead.

Twisted Beading Needles

Twisted beading needles have a huge loop eye and are constructed of flexible wire. On silk thread or ribbon cord, they are ideal for stringing pearls and gemstones. Because they are too flexible to follow a path through several beads, they are not suitable for off-loom bead weaving.

Because the huge eye collapses around the thread once it passes through the bead hole, twisted beading needles are difficult to reuse. In addition, they bend and flex far more than other needles.

Milliners Needles

Milliners' needles are comparable to English beading needles, with the exception that they are more accessible in sewing supply stores.

Milliners' needles are slightly thicker and have a more rounded eye than English beading needles.

Off-loom beadwork, loom beading, and bead embroidery can all be done with them.

Glovers Needles

Glovers' needles are used to stitch seed beads to leather, suede, and other thick textiles. They have a triangle-shaped pointy tip that easily penetrates leather and are sharper than conventional beading needles. Glovers' needles, like English beading needles, come in a number of sizes.

Choosing the Right Size Needles and Threads

One critical aspect of the success of your beading projects is choosing the correct needle and thread size for your seed beads. Because seed beads come in a variety of sizes and shapes, choosing the proper needle and thread for your project can make it easier and more pleasurable.

To allow for multiple thread passes through each bead, a smaller seed bead will necessitate a smaller thread and needle. Larger seed beads can be utilized with larger needles and thread, allowing for multiple additional thread passes without breaking.

In general, the smaller the bead and the bead hole, the greater the number of the size of the bead. In the same way, the thinner the needle is, the higher the number. This means that it can be used with smaller beads. Thread sizes vary by brand; however, Nymo is available in sizes ranging from "OO" (i.e., the thinnest) to "G" (i.e., the thickest). Nymo is available in the following sizes: OO, O, B, and D.

There are many various varieties of beading needles that have varied properties such as being more flexible, having a larger eye, and so on, in addition to varying sizes.

For Size 15 Seed Beads

Some of the smallest beads you can buy are size 15 seed beads.

These tiny beads work well with English beading needles in sizes 13 and 12. Use the thinnest needle size you are comfortable with if you choose to use milliners' needles.

With tiny size 15 seed beads, lightweight nylon threads work best. Nymo in sizes O and OO, as well as lighter weights of C-Lon, are excellent choices. Even the lightest weights of gel-spun threads, such as Fireline, will only allow one or two thread passes through these tiny beads. Therefore, use them for peyote stitch or brick stitch and avoid square stitch and right-angle weave.

For Sizes 10 and 11 Seed Beads

Seed beads in size 11 are the most usually available sizes. Seed beads in size 10 are slightly larger than size 11 beads. Size 11 beads are available from a variety of brands and manufacturers, and the holes on the beads can vary significantly in size.

The ideal needles to use with size 11 seed beads are English beading needles in sizes 10 and 12. If you need to maneuver through a tight spot, you can use a size 10 sharps or short beading needle. Bigeye and twisted beading needles may also be used, although their slightly larger size will limit the number of threads passes possible.

These beads work well with nylon beading threads in medium to heavy weights. You can also use to great success, gel-spun threads, or fishing line type threads. The stitch will eventually determine whether or not you use a smaller beading needle because thicker threads allow for fewer passes through each bead.

For Size 8 Seed Beads

Seed beads in size 8 are much larger than seed beads in size 11.

A size 12 or 10 English beading needle will readily fit size 8 seed beads. Because they allow for multiple passes through each bead, twisted beading needles and big eye needles work nicely with these larger beads.

These beads work well with heavyweight nylon beading threads. These beads also work well with gel-spun or fishing line threads, as their bigger holes allow for multiple passes through each bead without risking breaking it.

For Size 6 Seed Beads
Seed beads of size 6 are exceptionally large for seed beads,

with huge holes to allow needles and thread of larger sizes.

These beads work nicely with needles of size 10, as their bigger holes allow for multiple thread passes. Additionally, twisted beading needles, big eye needles, and the larger sizes of milliners' needles are also viable options.

Size 6 beads work well with heavyweight nylon beading threads. Threads of gel-spun or fishing line type in weights up to 10-pound test not only work well, but also support the weight of these beads. Because these beads typically have larger holes, multiple thread passes can be made without fear of shattering the beads.

Threading a Beading Needle

Threading beading needles may be more difficult than sewing needles owing to their thinness, flexibility, and smaller eyes. The beading needle eye is nearly the same thickness as the needle itself in order to make as many passes through a bead as possible. Getting your thread through the tiny eye of a beading needle can be frustrating as a result.

Threading your beading needle, on the other hand, does not have to be complicated. To find out what works best for you, try a few of these ideas and experiment with different types of needles and thread.

For a beginner, threading a beading needle can be difficult. If you believe a needle threader designed for standard sewing thread will suffice, think again—the eye is considerably smaller and will not function. Nevertheless, there are a few procedures you can take to thread your beading needle:

1. **Flatten the end**: Before trying to thread the needle with a thread like Fireline, Wildfire, or Nymo, flatten the thread ends. You

can do this with a jewelry-making plier or by running the end through your front teeth.

2. **Bring the needle to the end of the thread**: Try bringing the needle's eye to the thread instead of forcing the thread through the needle. This is often the reverse of how you see doing it, yet it works better.

3. **Be patient**: Even the most experienced beaders occasionally have difficulty threading their needles. When threading your needle

for the first few times, be patient.

4. **Invest in a specialized needle threader**:

    Invest in a needle threader designed exclusively for beading needles if all else fails. These can be found in craft and bead supply stores as well as online.

Good Lighting and a Solid Background

More than you might imagine, the appropriate setting can help. You can see the thread and needle eye more clearly in a well-lit room with a solid background that contrasts with your thread. Magnifying glasses come in handy when doing beadwork, especially when threading needles.

Prepare the Beading Thread

Depending on the type of thread you're using, threading the needle may be slightly different.

Condition nylon bead thread, such as Nymo, before attempting to thread your needle. Thread conditioner can be applied to the end of the thread that will be threaded through the needle. This will help to keep the nylon thread's fibers together, and reduce the likelihood of them splitting. At an angle, snip the thread's end.

Flatten the end of the thread tip before trying to thread the needle with gel-spun or braided/bonded fishing line types of beading thread like Fireline, WildFire, DandyLine, and PowerPro. You can flatten the thread end by pressing it between flat nose pliers, using your nails, or running the tip between your closed teeth. When the thread is flattened, it is easier to get through the needle's elongated eye.

Needle Threading Technique

It's time to start the procedure now that your thread is ready. The majority of individuals attempt to push a lengthy thread end through the eye of the needle. Now you need to do the opposite and push the eye of the needle onto the thread.

Hold the thread between your thumb and index finger with a small portion extending past your fingers, around two to four millimeters. Push onto the thread that has been flattened, or conditioned, the eye of the needle. It will usually slide on easily the first time.

But if you try more than once, and the thread won't go through the eye, turn the needle and try threading it through the other side of the eye. One side of the eye may be smoother than the other due to the way needles are made. This tiny distinction can alter the ease of threading the needle.

Needle Threading Tips

Thread many needles with lengths of beading thread once you've mastered threading your needle. It's useful to have a supply of pre-threaded needles on hand. Multiple needles should be threaded with lengths of beading thread, and the needle should be slid halfway down the thread. You can bead whenever the mood strikes after taping the threaded needles to a piece of cardboard or a surface from which they can be readily removed.

Another tip is that sewing supply stores sell tools called "needle threaders" that can help you thread your needle. When threading sewing needles, needle threaders are also utilized. Ensure that the only needle threaders you purchase are those designed specifically for beading needles. Threaders designed for sewing needles will not work with their smaller eye.

Finally, remember that practice is the key to getting better at anything. Threading your needle will become easier as you practice more.

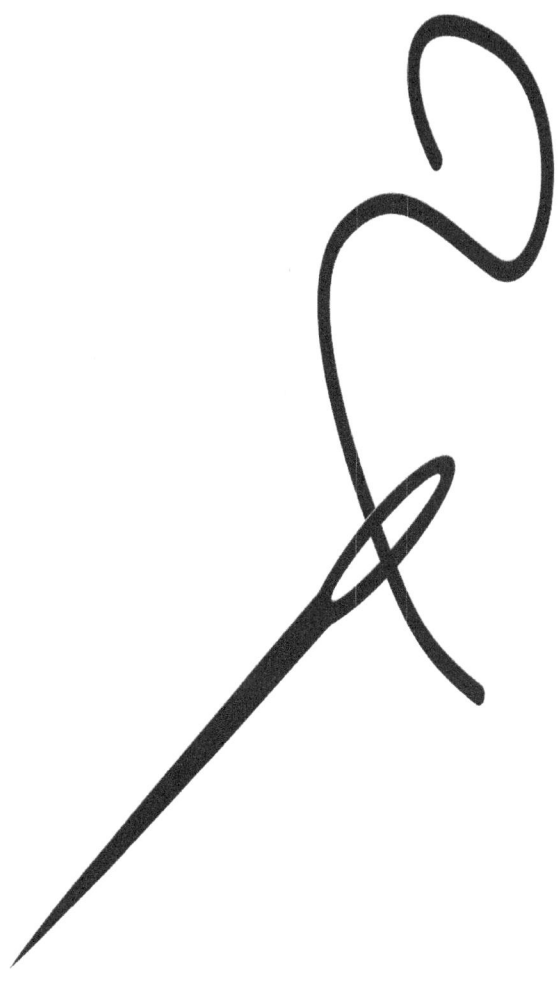

CHAPTER FIVE

MISTAKES TO AVOID AS BEGINNERS

If you get started on the proper road, beading can be an enjoyable, calming, and delightfully creative hobby with endless possibilities. I've compiled a list of typical beading errors, as well as some recommendations on how to avoid them, to assist you in that direction.

Using the Wrong Beads for a Project

It's tempting to get right into a beading project or a pattern with whatever beads you have on hand when you're just getting started.

This works occasionally, but not always. The beadwork might not lay flat or keep the shape you want it to; beads may appear to be improperly spaced; or your finished design may simply not look right for no apparent reason.

A good example is loom beadwork, which always looks more uniform when done with Japanese cylinder beads.

Consider whether the underlying cause is your beads before blaming it on poor technique. If you use beads that are even slightly different in size, shape, or manufacturer than those specified in a project's directions, your beadwork will look different from the sample. This is due to the fact that tiny changes in bead geometry are amplified by the enormous number of beads in the majority of beadwork. Using a bigger bead size than specified in the project instructions, for example, can have a significant impact on the project's thread tension.

You'll learn to choose acceptable alternative beads for the tasks and patterns you find as you gain experience. Meanwhile, adhere as closely as possible to the project instructions or make replacements only where the project calls for alternative types of beads.

Beading with Excessive Amount of Thread

The prospect of having to stop several times mid-project to add more beading thread irritates beginner beaders the most.

You could try stitching with a long-lasting, extra-long piece of thread, to avoid this. Unfortunately, the extra length has its own set of disadvantages.

It can snag on everything, from your shoelaces to the corner of your work table, for starters. Second, longer threads tangle more easily than shorter threads.

The time you save by switching threads less frequently can quickly outweigh the time you save pulling out tangles and picking at knots.

In the beginning, the extra-long thread increases the amount of effort required for each stitch, which is another problem with it. To complete a single stitch in beading, you must pull the thread through a bead, stop, pull the thread again, halt, and maybe pull the thread again. When working with a shorter thread, one or two pulls are sufficient for each stitch, resulting in a quicker completion of the job.

Finally, the longer thread is susceptible to greater wear as it is dragged through the beads, which can lead it to break either during the beading process or after the item is completed.

What's the answer? Begin by, at a time, pulling an arm's length of thread. Take your time when it comes to adding new threads; you'll get used to it.

Incorrect Beading Thread Tension

The way your beading drapes are affected by thread tension. Beadwork curls or puckers when tension is too tight, and it is floppy and may appear to have holes when tension is too slack.

It's impossible to avoid the truth that achieving the perfect thread tension requires practice. You can, however, speed up the process by forming excellent habits early on. Most crucial, practice gently tugging on the thread after each stitch is completed. For jobs that require "tight" tension, you can make that a forceful tug.

Also, take note of how your beadwork handling affects thread tension. You may discover, for instance, that when you halt and set down your beading, the tension eases. To avoid leaving a slack area with gaps between beads, give the thread a few tugs before you start stitching again.

Although excessively tight thread tension is permanent, tension that is too lax is frequently correctable.

Splitting of Your Beading Thread

When your beading needle accidentally passes through the thread in your beadwork, thread-splitting happens. Instead of snapping into place and lying flat, the last stitched bead can be caused to twist. Split thread also causes weak spots in your beading, and makes tearing out beadwork to correct a mistake more difficult.

Fortunately, most beadweaving beads have big holes that allow many, clean thread passes. Position your needle as far away as possible from the existing thread within each bead to avoid thread splitting.

Being Scared of Trying New Beadwork Stitches

There are several stitches and techniques to master in beadweaving, and not all of them will become favorites of yours. However, avoid developing stitch phobias, when you avoid learning a beadweaving stitch because you believe it would be difficult; thus, limiting yourself.

Odd-count flat peyote stitch is often feared by beginners. Some believe that weaving around the beads to reposition the needle will be much more difficult, especially when contrasted to the ease with which even- count flat peyote may be stitched. Odd-count flat peyote, on the other hand, allows you to do things like center motifs and make-shaped beading that would be difficult or impossible to do otherwise. Avoiding this stitch can severely limit your inventiveness.

Select the stitches you wish to learn depending on the outcomes they provide. If you appreciate the potential of a stitch, you should explore it. Just be patient and remember that every beadweaving thread is achievable. And with practice, even the most difficult techniques will become simpler.

Know that instead of expecting a perfect piece of beaded jewelry when you first start a new stitch, you should produce a practice piece.

CHAPTER SIX

HOW TO USE A BEAD LOOM

For the purpose of this tutorial, we'll be creating a tribal pattern.

Supplies

- Beading Needle
- Bead Loom
- Scissors
- Thread
- Seed Beads

Instructions

Step 1:   Prepare the Loom

1. We have to set up the warp threads first. Determine the width of your design. I've decided to make a strip that's seven beads wide (choose an odd number so

you get a 'one bead' point in the center if you want to make triangular shapes). The number of warp threads required is calculated by adding one to the number of beads.

2. Cut and knot together at the ends into loops, eight lengths of threads about a meter long.

3. To tighten the threads and produce tension, hook the loops onto the loom's wooden barrels and roll. Separate each thread into its own space on the coil between the barrels. A crochet hook is an extremely useful instrument for dividing strands.

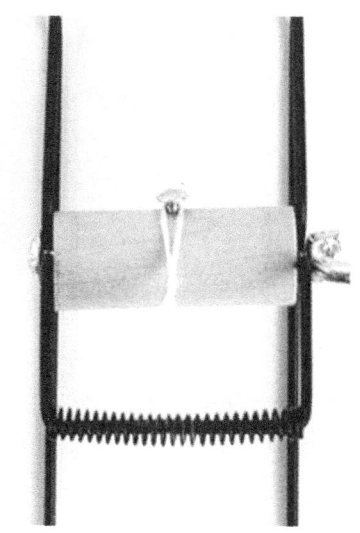

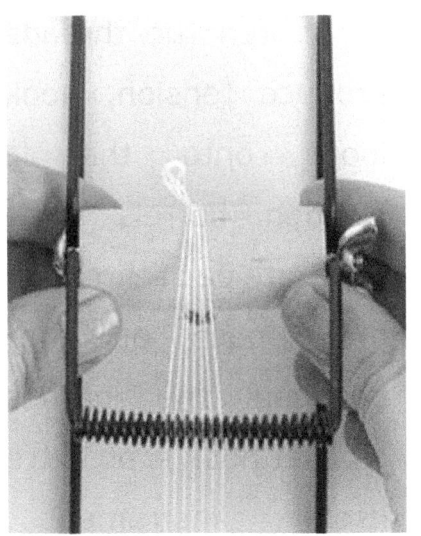
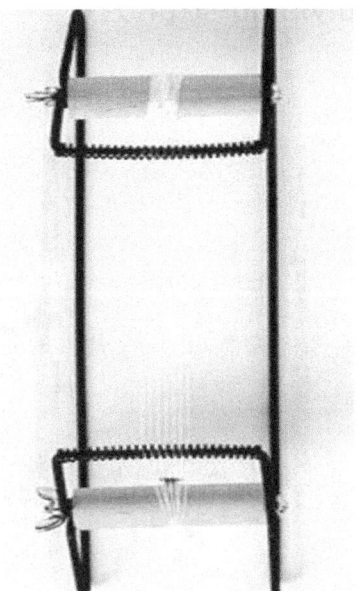

Step 2: Start Weaving

1. Use a long piece of thread to thread your needle. If you don't want to have to replace your weft too frequently, cut a long but manageable piece of thread.

2. Thread the needle with the first row of beads. They should not be moved down the thread. For the time being, just keep them on the needle.

3. Place the needle on top of the warp threads, and position the beads so that each one is sandwiched between two warp threads.

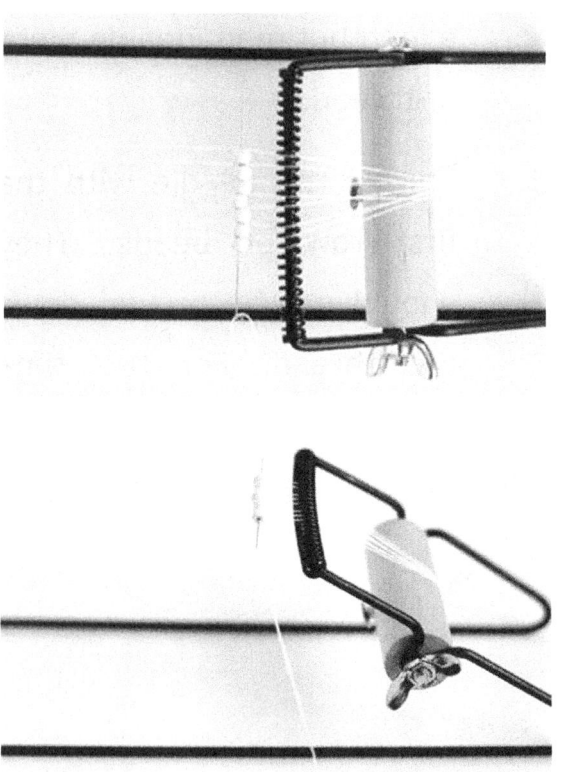

Pull the needle through the beads while holding the beads in place with your finger. Allow a lengthy thread tail to hang from the front bead.

4. Thread your needle back through the beads, after turning it around. As you thread through the holes in the beads, make sure the needle goes underneath each of the warp threads.

Pull the needle all the way through while holding the beads steady with your finger. This completes the first row! To make the second row, repeat steps three and four.

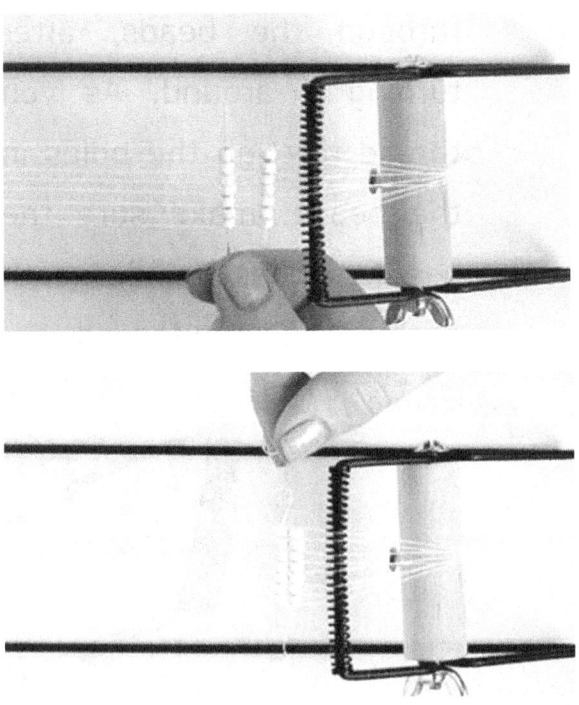

Step 3: Build Up Your Design

1. Continue to repeat these procedures, but vary the color and placement of the beads to build up your design.

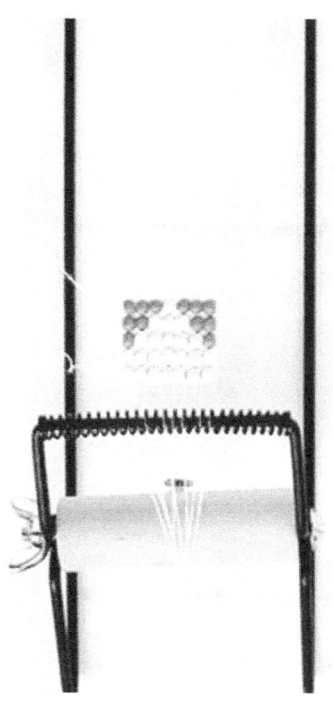

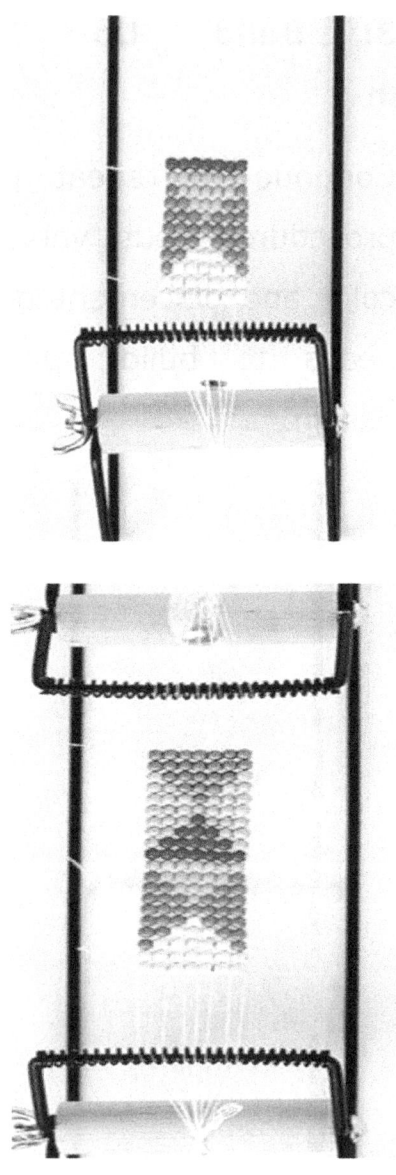

Step 4: Removing Your Work from Your Loom

1. Remove your design from the loom once you're satisfied with it. It is crucial that you remember this part! All of your hard work producing the design will come apart if you don't thread your warp threads correctly, leaving you with a beaded mess! To secure the beads, weave your weft (i.e., needle) thread back up and down through them.

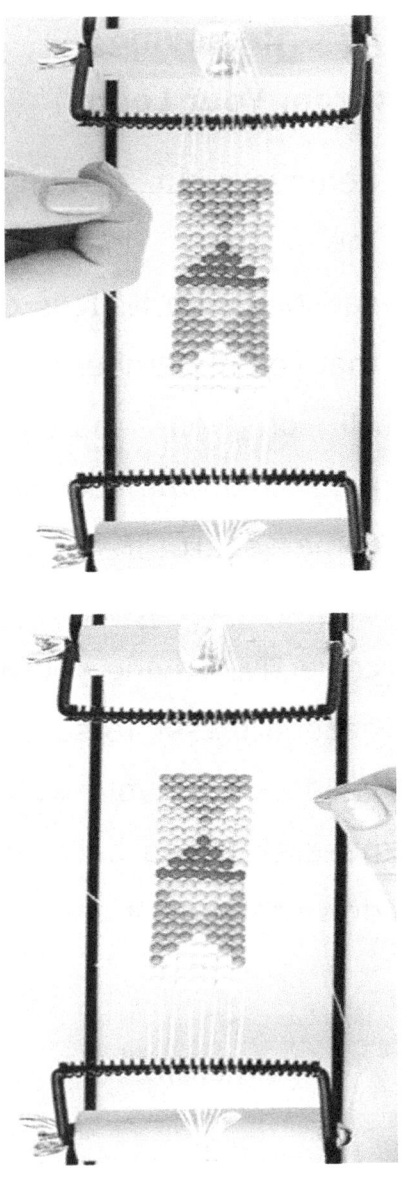

Cut the surplus thread in the center of a row after threading a few rows up. The thread is concealed within the work this way.

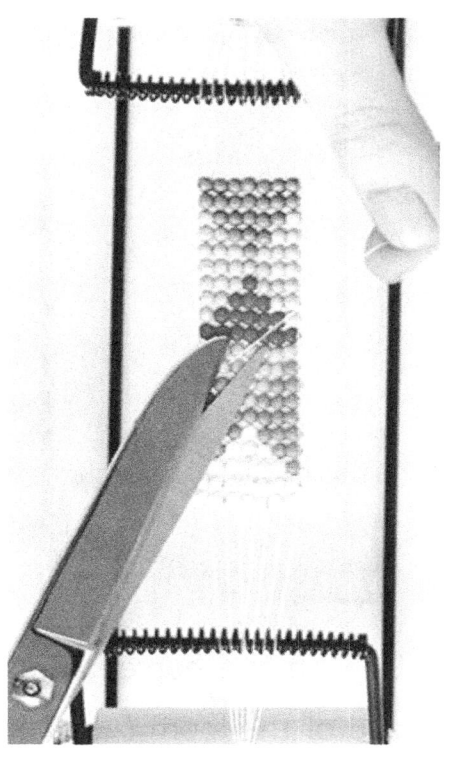

With the thread "tail" we left at the start of the piece, do the same thing.

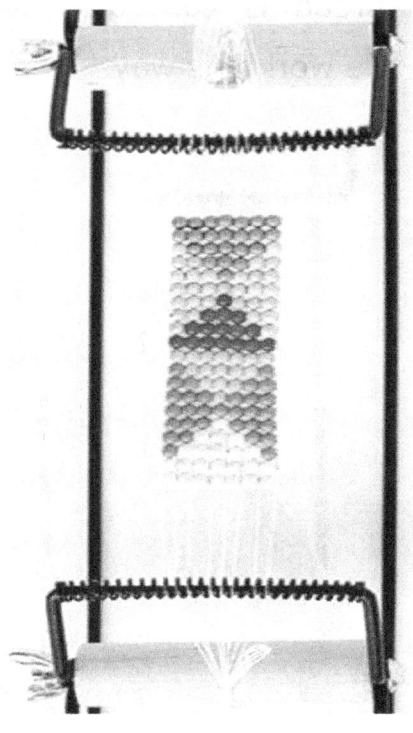

2. Unwind the barrel from one end of the loom (you can do this at any of the ends) to

loosen the threads a little. Cut the thread to a length of approximately 15 centimeters or 6 inches, on the far right.

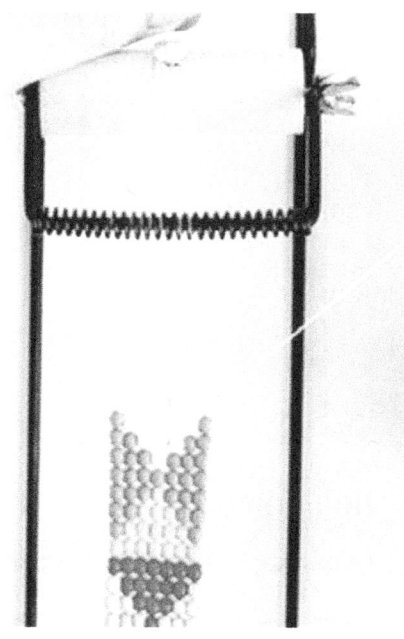

Thread the loose right thread onto a needle after

re-tightening the remaining warp threads.

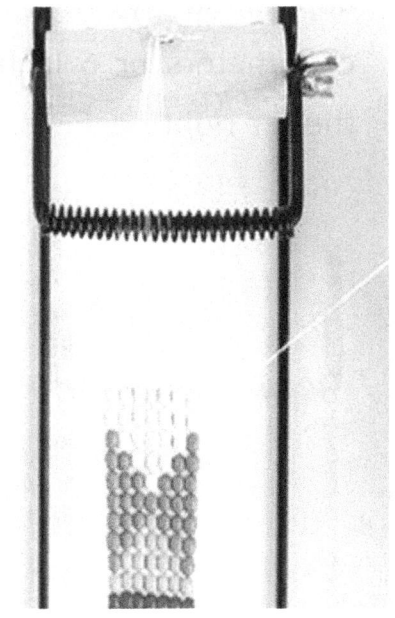

Beginning by going through the first two beads of the first row, and back through the first two beads of the second row, weave this thread into the pattern.

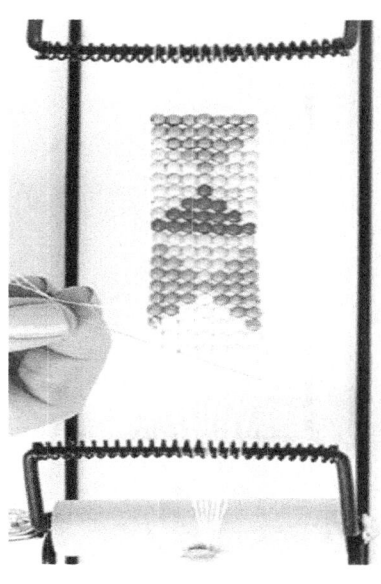

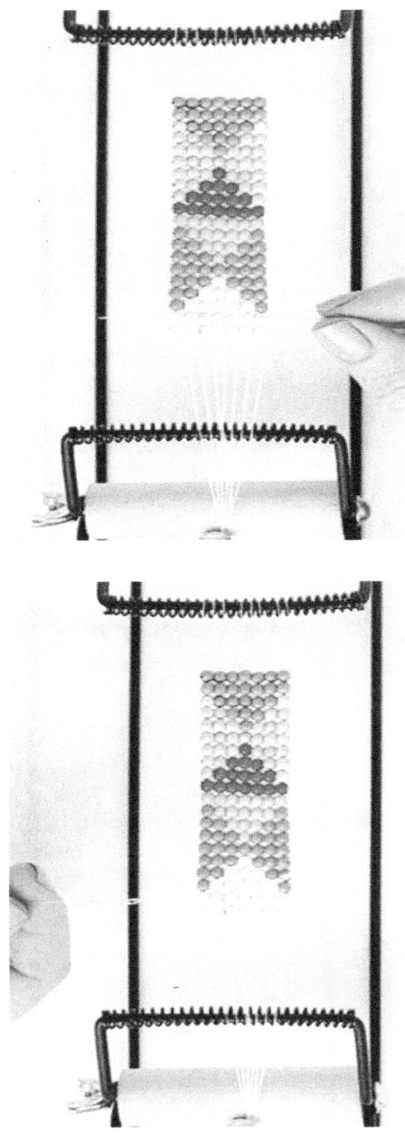

Cut off the excess warp thread after you've threaded it continuously through two beads in each row until you run out of thread.

3. In exactly the same manner as the previous one, cut the next warp thread from the loom.

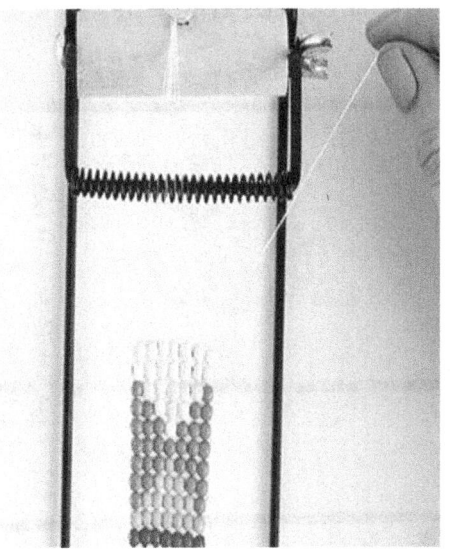

Next, start threading it into your work just like you did with the previous one. You'll move through the second and third beads from the end of each row this time.

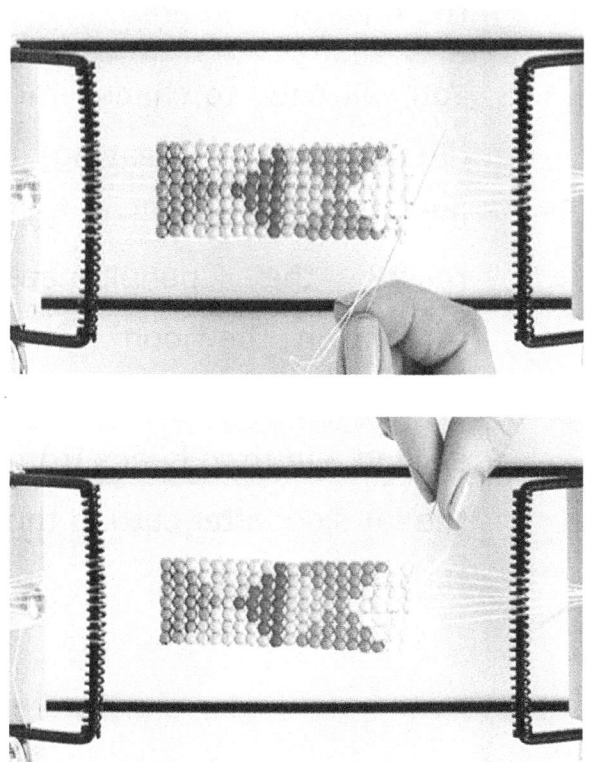

Continue performing similar actions with each warp thread, weaving each one–

in-one bead higher than the previous one, until you reach the final two threads.

4. You will need to change the direction you're weaving it into the beads, when you reach the penultimate thread on the loom. This time, weave through the second and third beads from the far side, after cutting the thread off the loom.

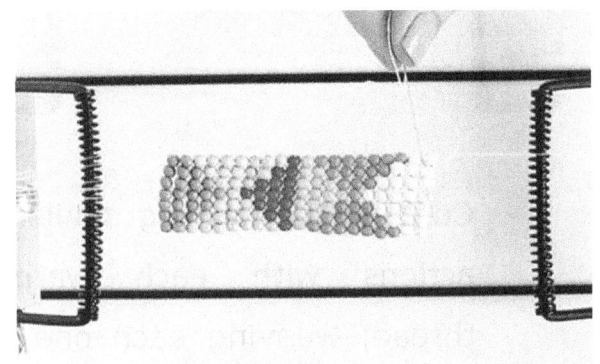

Then, return through the third and second beads of the following row. Continue as previously, and cut off any excess thread when the thread runs out.

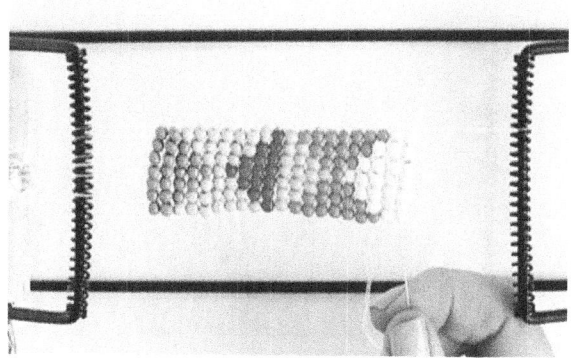

5. Cut it off the loom when you get to the last warp thread, and thread it through the first and second beads of each row while holding the work in your hand.

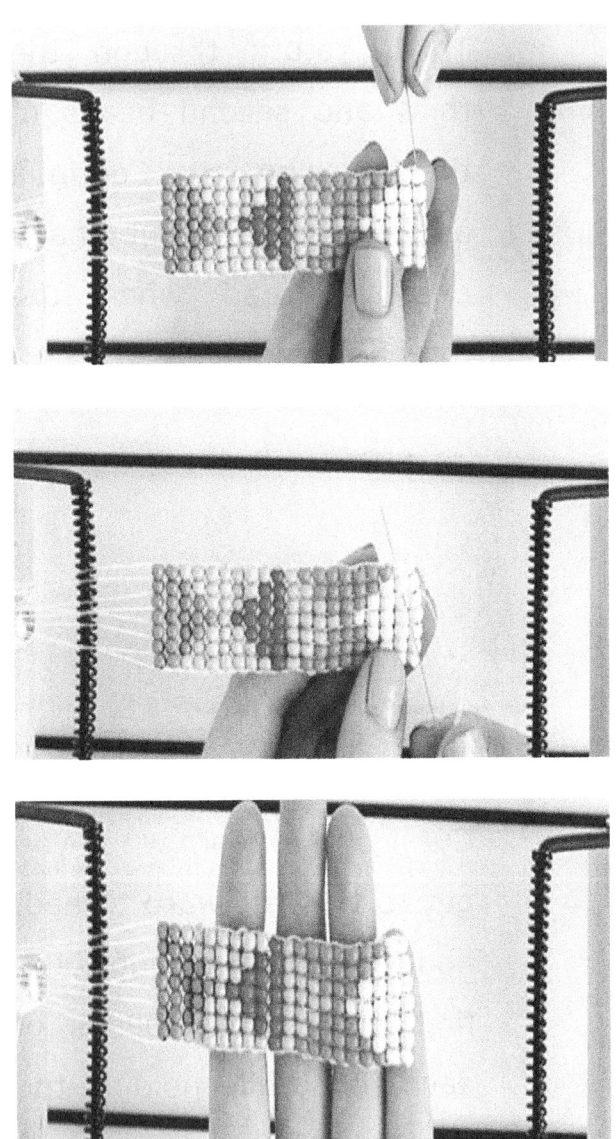

6. On the other side of the loom, repeat steps 2 – 5.

*

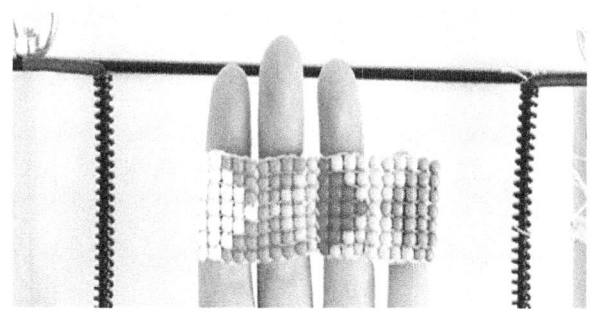

Your piece will be sturdy and ready to use once you're done threading your last warp thread.

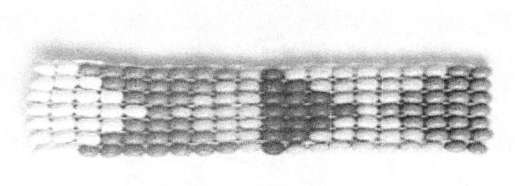

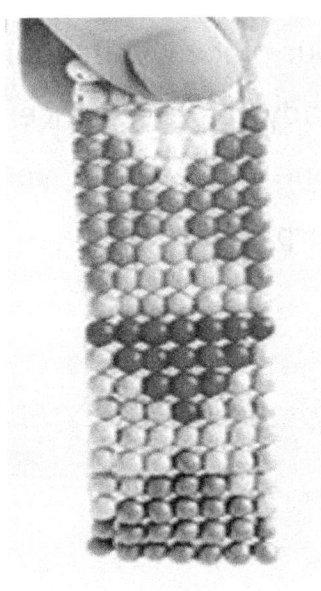

CHAPTER SEVEN

COMPLETING YOUR WORK

Slip Knots

This is known as buttonhole stitch among dressmakers. When this method is used, a new thread is always attached.

Note: There should never be a knot at the end.

Forming a full circle with the thread and then placing the needle into the center of the circle, scooping all the threads inside the circle, between the bead, the needle is exiting and the one about to be entered, is how a slip knot is produced. Tightly pull the thread up.

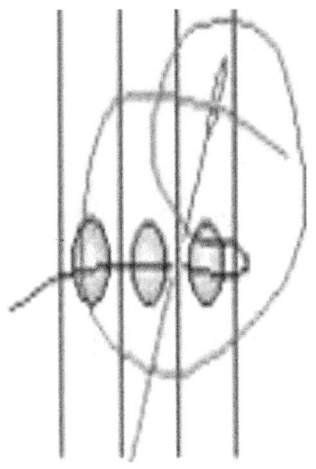

Decreasing

A decrease is accomplished by omitting the first and last warp threads on that row and the following rows, when the pattern specifies that the number of beads per row be decreased. This can be done as many times as necessary. After securing the warp threads with a slip knot at the end, work them into the beading.

Fringing

If there are enough warp threads left after the work has been removed from the loom, then, this can be done. There are two approaches:

Each strand of fringe is made from two warp threads. Thread the needle onto the end of the outside warp thread (i.e., left of bead A), after cutting the warp loops. Put the needle into bead B, then pass it down through the rest of the beads until you reach bead C.

Return up through bead C, as well as all the other beads, and knot onto the next warp thread after picking up beads D. Weave into the work, ends of the warp threads. The rest of the fringe strands are constructed in the same way.

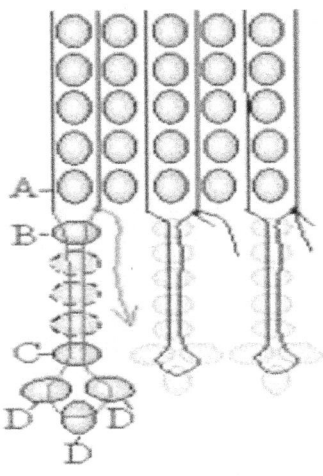

Thread the beads onto each warp thread for a closer fringe. Except the last three threaded, pass the needle back through all the beads. Use a slipknot to secure after working each warp thread back into the beadwork. Before cutting off the remaining thread, always pass the needle through a few beads.

Mounting Beadwork onto Other Material

To mount the beaded strip to felt, leather, ribbon, etc., or to attach Velcro to the edges, this method is used.

Weave a selvedge of at least one centimeter (i.e., ½ inch) onto the warp threads with the weft thread before removing the beadwork from the loom. The traditional 'under/over' darning method of weaving is used. Leave to dry after carefully spreading a thin layer of glue onto the reverse side of the thread woven section.

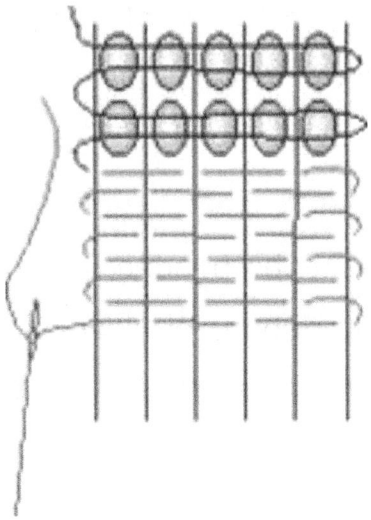

The warp threads can be clipped level with the end of the weaving once the work is removed from the loom. Then, the warp threads can either be folded under and/or bonded in place between the beading and the backing fabric, depending on your preference. Stitch all along the long edges of the piece, with a matching thread through the side warp threads of the beading and the backing material. Sew through all layers one bead row in from the edge to secure the short ends.

Joining Two Pieces of Beadwork

This is a job for two people. Cut the warp loops open after removing the beading parts from the loom.

The 'helper' takes a pair of warp threads, one from each side, and ties them tightly together twice, while the other person is holding the right sides together. From the knot, cut 1 centimeter or ½-inch. With each successive pair of warp threads, repeat this process.

Glue a small strip of felt onto the reverse side of the beadwork to hide the joint, after applying a little layer of glue or clear nail varnish to these knots.

Threading each warp thread in turn, onto a needle and working it into the opposite end of the other piece of beadwork is a more elaborate and neater procedure. Slipknot each thread to secure.

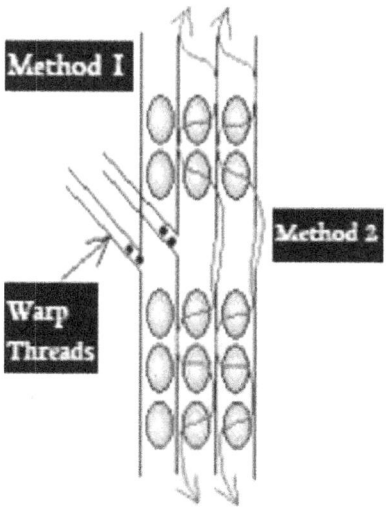

Side Fringing

To produce a 6-bead side fringe, follow these steps:

Thread on a row of beads in the usual manner, following the pattern, after tying the weaving thread onto the first left-hand warp thread, but for the side fringe, add six extra beads. Ignore the sixth bead when turning at the end of the row, and then work through the pattern beads as usual after threading the weaving thread back through the 5 fringe beads.

Proceed in this manner until the specified number of fringe strands have been worked, and after that, carry on working the main strip of beading on the warp threads.

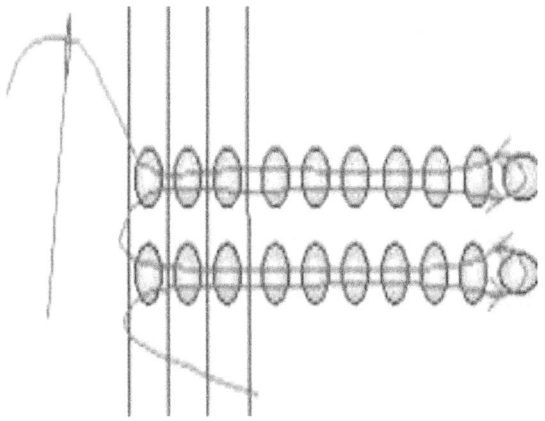

Selvage Method

Weaving a selvage edge keeps threads from coming apart. The weft thread is used to stitch the warp threads into a selvage at either end of your loom beading using the selvage method of finishing up your loom beadwork. Then, to make a bracelet like the one shown here, you can sew the selvage onto fabric, glue it to the back of your beadwork, or put it inside the ends of a ribbon clamp.

This tutorial shows how to finish with a fixed frame or upright bead loom that doesn't have a shedding device. If you use an upright loom that is equipped with a shedding device, the technique will be slightly different.

The Materials

The following items are required to complete your beading using the selvage method described in this tutorial:

For Loom Beadwork

- Beading needle
- Beads
- Weft threads or cords
- A Loom
- A warp
- Embroidery scissors

Using the Selvage Method for Beadwork:

- E6000 or UV coating or epoxy resin of your preference
- Toothpick for applying glue or resin
- Jump rings and a clasp of your chosen
- Paper towels
- Two pairs of flat nose or chain nose pliers, or one pair of each, are required to attach the jump rings and clasp
- Nylon jaw pliers

- Two ribbon clamp ends, each with a length that matches the width of your beading

One way to seal selvages is with UV resin, which hardens quickly under UV light, is strong, and doesn't give off strong smells or fumes. If you don't want to work with resin, you might try using E6000 adhesive instead.

Instructions

Leave Enough Weft Thread Tail for a Selvage End

When you finish off using the selvage method, you should start your beadwork with a weft thread tail that is extra-long. Weaving the selvage requires the use of the long tail.

In other words, the length of the weft thread should be equal to the length of your selvage tail (approximately 30 inches) plus the length of thread you choose to use for looming your beading.

You are able to apply the selvage technique even if you fail to remember to leave a long weft thread tail. You will merely need to return to the end of your beading, and add a new weft thread to the end of it before you can proceed with making the selvage.

Tie a Half Hitch Knot After Completing Your Loom Beadwork

Weave the complete beadwork design on the loom as you normally would. Tie a half hitch knot around the last warp thread or cord with the weft thread once you've finished your final row of beadwork.

Begin the Weaving of the Selvage

The needle should be woven underneath the last warp thread, and up over the subsequent warp thread. Carry on working your way toward the end of the row, weaving over and under as you go. Picking is the term for this action.

Another thread row is woven. Slide down each row of thread with your fingers toward your beading.

Finish the First Selvage

Carry on with the process of weaving until you have accumulated sufficient selvage to entirely occupy the space contained within one of your ribbon clamps ends. About 30 passes with the weft thread were required in my sample.

Over the final warp thread, tie a half–hitch knot to complete the selvage.

Proceed to the Weaving of the Second Selvage

At the other end of the beadwork, thread the needle onto the long thread tail and weave a matching selvage.

Apply Resin or Glue to the Two Selvages

With a coat of E6000 or coating resin, cover the upper surface of each selvage while your beadwork is still on the loom.

Mixing two equal parts of resin and hardener is required to make epoxy coating resins like Envirotex Lite. After that, you either pour it on or paint it on, and then you wait for it to cure for at least 24 hours.

Spread the glue or resin while it is still wet, over the entire selvage, using a toothpick. Before taking the item from the loom, you should give the glue or resin sufficient time to completely dry.

Cut Beadwork off of Loom

Using embroidery scissors, cut the warp threads on either side of the selvage to remove the beading from the loom.

You can use the same pair of scissors to trim the warps so that they are flush with both selvages, and then you can cut off any leftover weft tails after the glue or resin has had enough time to completely dry.

Glue Clamps Ends to Selvages

The next step is to apply to the ends of the selvages, with the clamp ends off of the selvages, some E6000.

Center the clamp ends on your beadwork after sliding them on. To remove any extra glue that oozes out, use a paper towel to wipe it off. Due to the adhesive's rubbery nature, excess glue can be picked off once it begins to dry.

Allow the glue to cure for around 24 hours by setting aside your beadwork again.

Ribbon Clamp Ends Addition

Make the holes in each of your clamps a little bit smaller by using nylon jaw pliers to gently squeeze down on each of the clamp ends.

The clamp ends should be just broad enough so that they may glide over your selvages, but you should not adjust them while they are on the selvages unless the clamp ends do not have serrations. Your selvage can be readily hacked through by clamp ends that have serrations, which can potentially cause your design to break apart.

Apply Glue to Ribbon Clamps

A very small amount of E6000 glue should be applied to the interior of the ribbon clamps. As a result, the selvage will be kept securely within the ribbon clamps.

Set the Ribbon Clamp in Place

Slide into place, on the selvage end, the ribbon clamp. It is very important to make sure that all selvage is adequately covered and that the beads are outside of the ribbon clamp, particularly if you are dealing with smaller beads that could potentially be shattered when the ribbon clamp is closed.

Close Ribbon Clamp

After the ribbon clamp has been positioned to the loom beading in the correct manner, use the nylon jaw pliers to close them around the selvage carefully and securely. Pliers with nylon jaws are required to be used if one wishes to avoid marring the surface of the ribbon clamps.

Beadwork will have a clean and professional-looking finish thanks to the ribbon clamps that firmly grip the selvage. The cords will not come apart or fray as a result of this.

Clasp Attachment

Attach a clasp to your clamp ends with jump rings using pliers, once the ribbon clamps' adhesive has had time to cure.

Adding a length of jewelry chain between one clamp end and the clasp part will allow you to lengthen your bracelet if it is too short. You may also make the bracelet clasp more easily by attaching a charm or dangle to the chain.

CHAPTER EIGHT
BEAD LOOM PRACTICE PATTERN

Miyuki Bead Loom Cuff Bracelet

Supplies

- Bead loom – you can make use of a metallic bead loom if you desire.
- Beading thread – the Miyuki or Sono brands are great choices.
- A fine beading needle
- Miyuki delica 11/0 beads
- Jewelry glue such as Hasulith or E6000

- Cuff bracelet 15mm wide – could be in gold or silver color.

Instructions

Step 1: Prepare the Bead Loom

In preparing your bead loom, if you have an adjustable bead loom, you may be able to do the entire length of the bracelet. In this scenario, ensure that the distance between your two coils is at least the length of the bracelet plus 2 centimeters on both sides. The overall length of the cuff bracelet that I utilized was 16.5 centimeters, which is equivalent to 95 rows.

The next step is to secure your thread by tying a knot to the center screw that is situated on the wooden barrel that is located on one side of your bead loom. Pull your thread through the coil on the same side, slightly offset from the center, starting from this anchor point. Then make a loop around the center screw on that side after crossing it to the other side coil, and going through it.

Leave one spacer between this thread, and the previous one, and go through the center, after going through the coil. Leave one spacer between this thread and the previous one and make a loop around the screw, after crossing again to the other side. Until you have eight threads crossing the loom, keep going in this manner. Even if the explanations appear to be complicated, it is actually quite simple.

Before getting started, you should first roll the barrels to tension the threads using the screws that are maintaining the barrels. It is not necessary for it to be too tight, but the threads should be kept in position very well in order to keep a consistent beadwork.

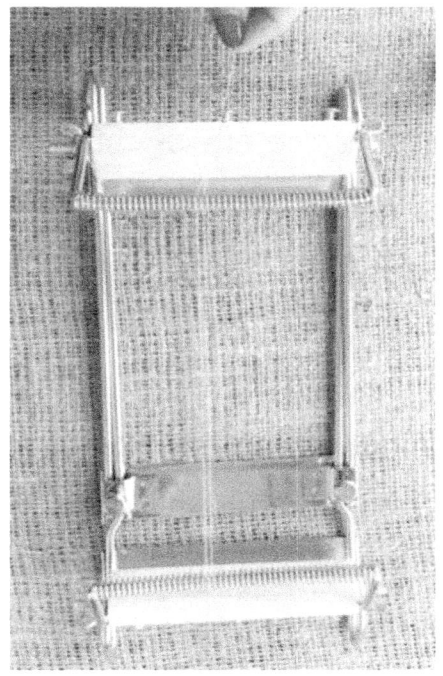

Step 2: Thread the Bead Row after Row

Prepare 2 meters of thread, and tie a basic knot about 5 cm from the coil on the first thread. After threading your needle, move it in one direction through the threads that have been installed on the loom, then return by passing the needle alternately above and below the threads. Perform this action twice more, and you are ready to begin.

Thread your beads according to the first row of the pattern. Go below the threads with your needle.

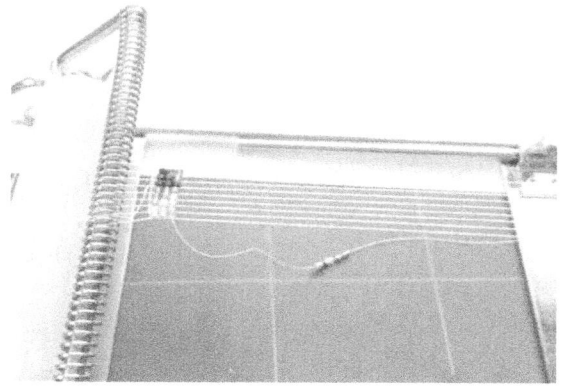

Then, keeping the beads in place from below, use your fingers to place them between each thread.

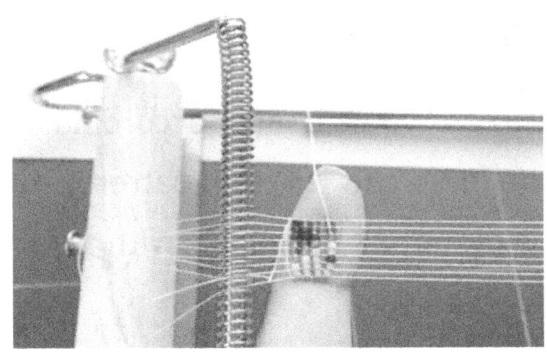

Thread all of the beads in this row once they're all in position. Above the loom's threads, your needle should go.

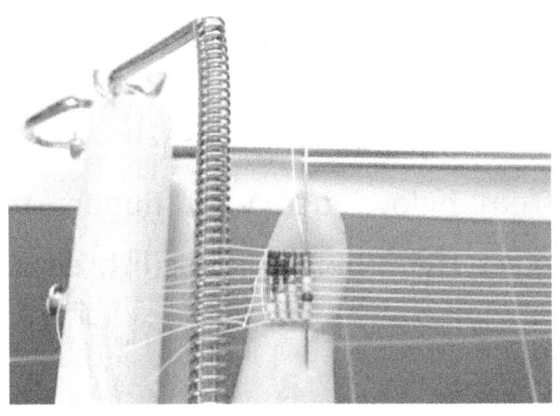

With this, your row is now fixed.

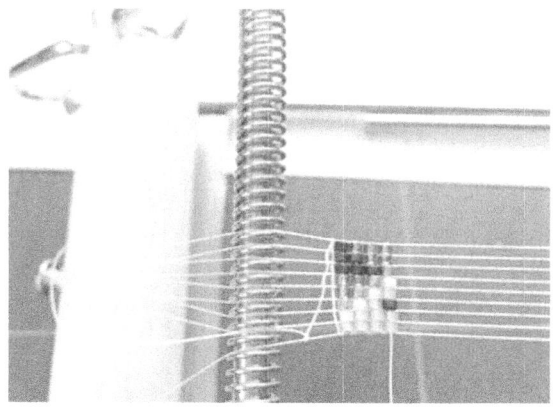

You may have observed that the photographs above show a pattern with eight beads per row. Since then, I've crafted a new bracelet using a pattern that calls for seven beads to be strung along each row in order to accommodate the cuff bracelet.

Then, for each row of your beadwork, repeat this approach. Check out how simple it is!

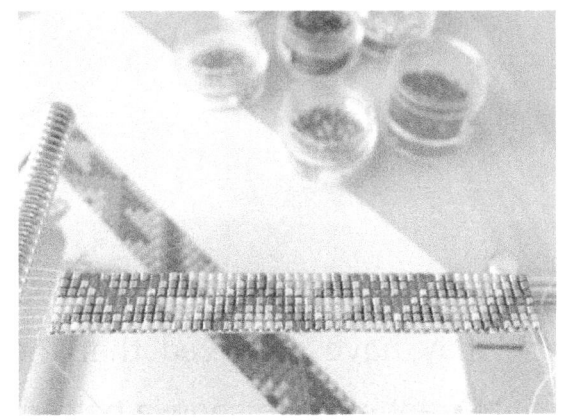

Step 3: Renew and/or Hide Your Thread

You may not have enough thread to finish the beadwork. Simply weave your thread back through the rows in such circumstance. Take a new thread, and weave through the rows until you reach the row you stopped on, starting about 5 rows before the row you stopped. You are free to carry on with your beadwork.

Simply weave your thread back through the previous rows to hide the end thread when you reach the end of your beadwork.

Remember those few thread-only rows you did at the start? To hide the thread, carefully remove the knot, thread your needle, and weave through the first rows.

Step 4: Release the Beadwork from the Loom

How do you get your beaded work off the loom?

This section may be tedious at times. So, be warned.

Making beautiful jewelry is not only enjoyable; there are also steps to take to ensure that your creation does not fall apart over time. The idea is to cut your threads as close to the screws as possible.

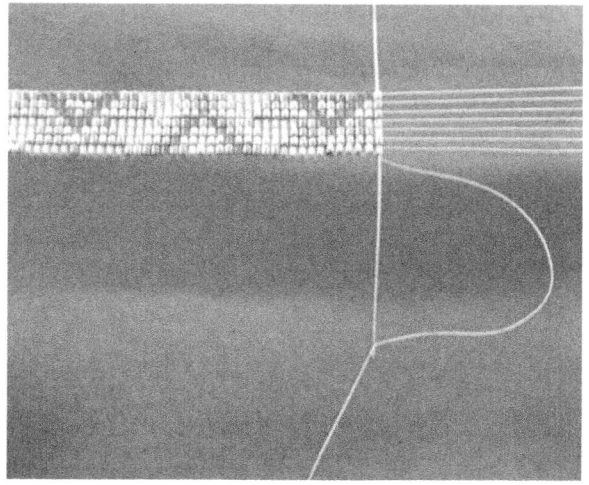

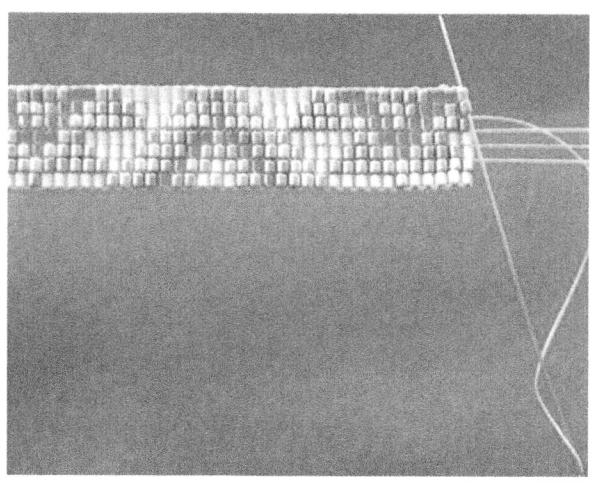

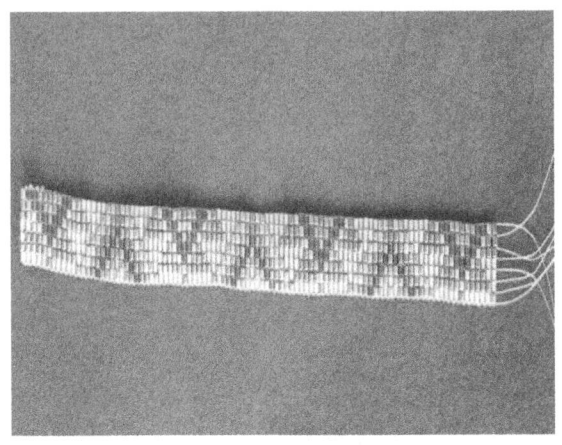

Weave through the work after threading your needle with one thread. To hide the threads, and ensure your ends will not fray in the future, you have to do this with all of the threads.

Step 5: Mount the Beadwork on the Cuff Bracelet

You have now finished the weaving. Before you mount it on

the cuff bracelet, double-check that you have the required number of rows and that it fits perfectly inside the area available! Although it seems ridiculous, I am completely aware of what I am discussing. After you have confirmed that, you may proceed to mount the weaving on the bracelet by using your magic glue.

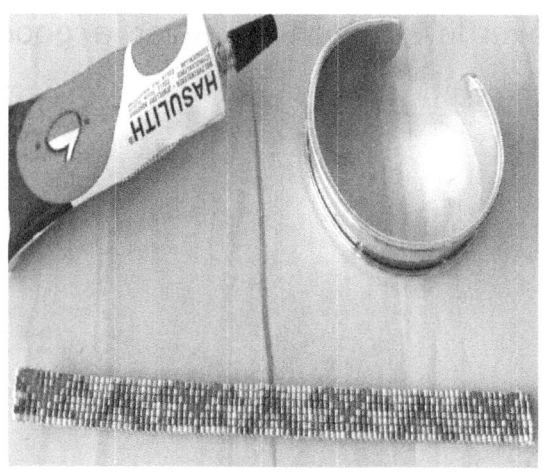

Apply some glue, starting at one end.

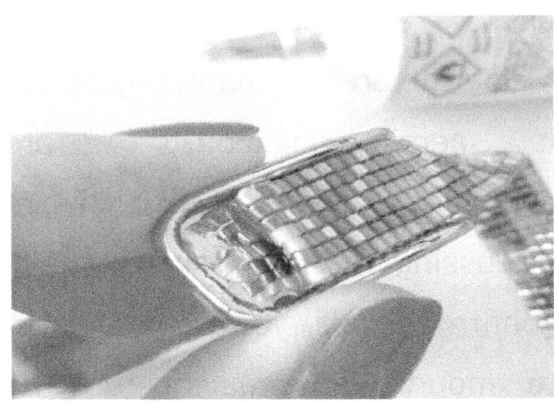

If you put too much, it will overflow, which is never a good thing.

Before wearing it, allow at least 24 hours for it to dry.

And so, using the bead looming technique, you have made a fantastic bracelet.

Three Beaded Bracelet Patterns

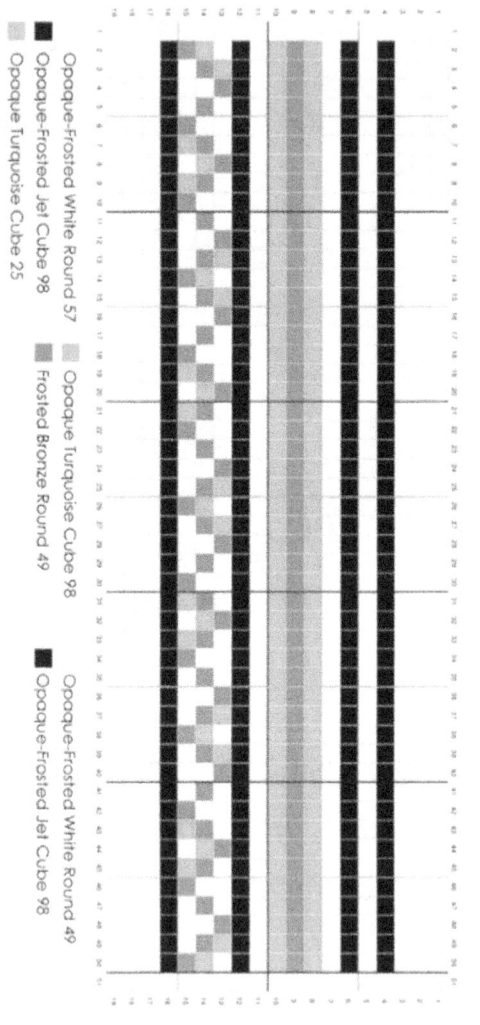

Make Your Own Pattern

On this website, https://www.stitchfiddle.com/en/chart/create, you can create your own pattern for free. The site is great since you can create a design in a matter of minutes, or even upload a photo and have it converted into a cross-stitch design that you can use for your bead weaving project.

Made in the USA
Las Vegas, NV
18 May 2024

90081793R00075